How Military Helicopters Work

Walt Brody

Lerner Publications • Minneapolis

Lerner Publications Company
A division of Lerner Publishing Group, Inc.
241 First Avenue North
Minneapolis, MN 55401 USA

For reading levels and more information, look up this title at www.lernerbooks.com.

Library of Congress Cataloging-in-Publication Data

Names: Brody, Walt, 1978- author.
Title: How military helicopters work / Walt Brody.
Description: Minneapolis, MN : Lerner Publications, [2020] | Series: Lightning bolt books.
    Military machines | Includes bibliographical references and index. | Audience: Grades K-3.
Identifiers: LCCN 2018044365 (print) | LCCN 2018045270 (ebook) | ISBN 9781541557437
    (eb pdf) | ISBN 9781541557406 (lb : alk. paper)
Subjects: LCSH: Military helicopters—Juvenile literature.
Classification: LCC UG1230 (ebook) | LCC UG1230 .B76 2020 (print) | DDC 623.74/60472—dc23

LC record available at https://lccn.loc.gov/2018044365

Manufactured in the United States of America
1-46151-45950-1/8/2019

Table of Contents

The Soaring Helicopter

Militaries need to move soldiers and equipment fast during missions. Flying in helicopters is a quick way to move people and things from one place to another.

Helicopters can stay in one place in the air.

Soldiers have missions all around the world. Helicopters can take off and land without a runway. They go many places that other vehicles cannot reach.

A helicopter uses rotor blades to fly. These blades spin very fast. They allow helicopters to move in any direction.

Some helicopters can carry more than fifty-five people.

Helicopters have one pilot. But they can have a copilot too. The copilot helps fly the helicopter.

A History of Helicopters

Leonardo da Vinci was an inventor. He had an idea for a flying machine in the 1480s. He never built it.

Igor Sikorsky's first helicopter was the VS-300.

In 1939, Igor Sikorsky made the first modern helicopter. A modern helicopter has rotor blades on top and on its tail.

Helicopters save lives during war by quickly getting soldiers medical care.

Military helicopters became common in the 1950s. They brought supplies to soldiers fighting in wars. Helicopters also brought injured soldiers to safety.

Parts of a Helicopter

The main rotor is on top of a helicopter. It connects to the helicopter's engine. The engine spins the main rotor's blades.

Helicopters also have a rotor on their tail. It spins to keep the helicopter balanced and help it turn.

On most helicopters, the tail rotor is much smaller than the main rotor.

Helicopters sit on landing skids when they are not flying. Some helicopters have floats so they can land on water.

The pilot sits in the cockpit.
He uses the controls to fly the
helicopter. Pedals on the floor
move the tail rotor.

A US Apache helicopter can carry many different types of missiles.

Some military helicopters have guns. They can carry missiles too.

Helicopters in Action

Soldiers use helicopters to watch targets from above. Cameras on the helicopters gather information about enemy forces.

Attack helicopters go on dangerous missions. They have armor that helps protect them. The rotor blades are made to keep working even after being shot.

Helicopters can help move injured people to safety.

Helicopters have other uses too. They rescue people who get injured or lost in hard-to-reach places.

The United States plans to send a helicopter to Mars in 2020. It will learn about the planet's air and weather. Helicopters will help us explore places we have never been to before!

A helicopter like this one could explore Mars without a pilot.

Helicopter Diagram

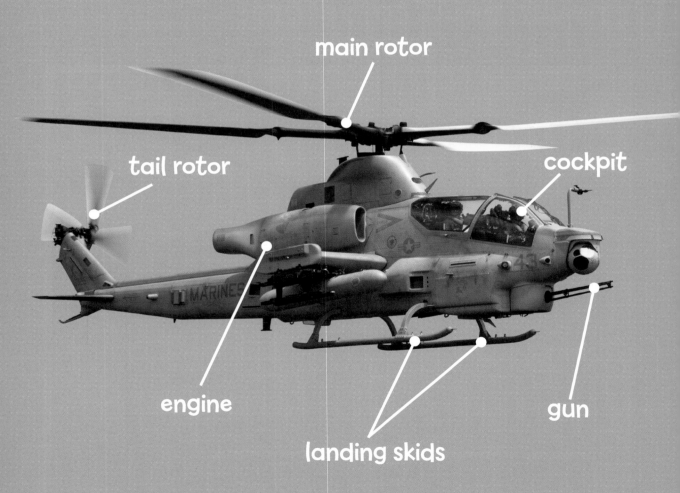

main rotor

tail rotor

cockpit

engine

gun

landing skids

Helicopter Facts

- Forest fires are dangerous. Helicopters fly over the fire and dump water on it. They help put the fire out.

- Helicopters have many nicknames. They are called choppers, copters, eggbeaters, and whirlybirds.

- A Skycrane helicopter is huge. The main rotor blades are 72 feet (22 m) across. It is big enough to carry a tank!

Glossary

cockpit: the place in a helicopter where the pilot sits

landing skid: a part of a helicopter that supports the helicopter's weight on the ground

missile: a rocket used to attack something far away

mission: an official assignment given to soldiers

pedal: a lever on the floor of a helicopter that controls the tail rotor

pilot: the person who flies a helicopter

rotor blade: a long piece of metal that spins to make a helicopter fly

runway: a long strip of ground used by airplanes to take off and land

Further Reading

Boothroyd, Jennifer. *Inside the US Air Force*. Minneapolis: Lerner Publications, 2018.

Fortuna, Lois. *Rescue Helicopters*. New York: Gareth Stevens, 2016.

Kiddle: Helicopter Facts
https://kids.kiddle.co/Helicopter

Riggs, Kate. *Helicopters*. Mankato, MN: Creative Education, 2015.

Science for Kids: Facts about Helicopters
http://www.scienceforkidsclub.com/helicopters.html

Science Kids: Helicopter Facts for Kids
http://www.sciencekids.co.nz/sciencefacts/vehicles/helicopters.html

Index

Photo Acknowledgments

Image credits: US Army photo by Wendy Brown, pp. copyright, 15; US Air Force photo by Senior Airman Katrina M. Brisbin, p. 4; US Air Force photo by Tech. Sgt. Lealan Buehrer, p. 5; US Air Force photo by T.C. Perkins Jr., p. 6; Tim Sloan/Staff/Getty Images, p. 7; Fratelli Alinari IDEA S.p.A./Contributor/Getty Images, p. 8; Bettmann/Contributor/Getty Images, p. 9; US Air Force photo, p. 10; US Air Force photo by Senior Airman Michael Washburn, p. 11; Lucas Rizzi/Shutterstock.com, p. 12; Greg Mathieson/Mai/Contributor/Getty Images, p. 13; Chung Sung-Jun/Stringer/Getty Images, p. 14; US Army Photo by Wendy Brown, p. 15; US Navy photo by Mass Communication Specialist 2nd Class Travis Litke, p. 16; US Army photo by Charles Rosemond, pp. 17, 23; US Coast Guard photo by Petty Officer 3rd Class Brian McCrum, p. 18; NASA/JPL-Caltech, p. 19; Smith Collection/Gado/Contributor/Getty Images, p. 20.

Cover photo: Smith Collection/Gado/Getty Images.

Main body text set in Billy Infant regular 28/36. Typeface provided by SparkType.